# THE LEGACY OF SIGMUND FREUD

Sigmund Freud, working on the manuscript of *Moses and Monotheism*

# THE LEGACY OF SIGMUND FREUD

*JACOB A. ARLOW, M.D.*

International Universities Press, Inc.

NEW YORK, 1956

# FREUD CENTENARY COMMITTEE
## The American Psychoanalytic Association

BERTRAM D. LEWIN, M.D., *Chairman*

K. R. EISSLER, M.D., *Secretary*

JACOB A. ARLOW, M.D.

BERNARD BANDLER, M.D.

R. S. BOOKHAMMER, M.D.

CHARLES BRENNER, M.D.

WINSTON I. BRESLIN, M.D.

BERNARD L. DIAMOND, M.D.

HARRY FREUD

MARCEL HEIMAN, M.D.

OTTO ISAKOWER, M.D.

NAOMI KATCHER, M.D.

ERNST KRIS, PH.D.

SYDNEY G. MARGOLIN, M.D.

EVA J. MEYER

WERNER NATHAN, M.D.

WILLIAM G. NIEDERLAND, M.D.

DOUGLASS W. ORR, M.D.

MARIAN C. PUTNAM, M.D.

LEWIS L. ROBBINS, M.D.

MARTIN H. STEIN, M.D.

FRANK VOGEL, M.D.

## *Ex-officio*

IVES HENDRICK, M.D.

JOHN N. MCVEIGH

## *The American Psychoanalytic Association Officers*

MAXWELL GITELSON, M.D.
*President*

WILLIAM G. BARRETT, M.D.
*President-Elect*

DOUGLAS D. BOND, M.D.
*Secretary*

ROBERT T. MORSE, M.D.
*Treasurer*

TO ALICE

# Contents

# Preface

THIS monograph grew out of the work of the Freud Centenary Committee of the American Psychoanalytic Association. It fell in my charge to arrange a display of Freud's work—directed to the general public rather than to the expert in psychoanalysis or in the history of science. The central theme of the exhibition of Freud's writings, as of this monograph, was to portray some measure of the genius of Sigmund Freud and of the rich legacy of his labors of which all mankind is the beneficiary. In keeping with this spirit, no all-encompassing evaluation of Freud and his impact on the twentieth century has been attempted. Such a work is beyond the scope of this study or the capacity of the author. A representative sampling of Freud's work, organized according to the various departments of his interest and correlated roughly with the different periods of his life, has been outlined. It is my hope that, from these pages, there will emerge an appreciation of the richness of Freud's genius, the development of his thought, and the manifold implications of his thought to the science of psychoanalysis of which he was the founder and the principal developer.

Acknowledgment is due to the members of the Freud Centenary Committee of the American Psychoanalytic Association who encouraged me in the writing of this essay; to Dr. Jacob Shatzky, librarian of the New York State Psychiatric Institute, for giving us access to many valuable items of Freudiana; and especially to Mrs. Eva J. Meyer, librarian of the New York Psychoanalytic Institute, for assembling the material, checking the bibliography, and for translating material otherwise inaccessible. Thanks are due the Freud Archives and the Hogarth Press; and to Basic Books, publishers of *The Origins of Psychoanalysis* and the *Life and Work of Sigmund Freud* by Ernest Jones for permission to quote from those sources. Finally, a particular note of acknowledgment is due Dr. A. S. Kagan of the International Universities Press for his splendid cooperation in the publication of this book.

Jacob A. Arlow, M.D.

*New York, N. Y.*

# 1.

# *Freud as a Biologist*

*"Nature has neither language nor speech, but she creates tongues and hearts through which she feels and speaks. . . . Her laws are unchangeable—she has few springs of action but they never wear out; they are always operative, always manifold. . . . Even the most unnatural things are natural."*

—GOETHE, ESSAYS ON NATURE

INSPIRED by a public reading of this essay, Sigmund Freud, who was at the time a young and brilliant student, decided to devote himself to biological research. He had been born on May 6, 1856 in the town of Freiburg in Moravia, then part of the Austrian empire. As the son of a middle-class Jewish businessman a career in some learned profession seemed to be his inevitable goal as an intellectual. His record in the lower forms had been exceptional, but not until the experience of the public reading of Goethe's essay was he able to resolve his indecision concerning his career and decide upon his life's work.

While still a student, Freud was awarded a research scholarship to a newly established marine biological laboratory at Trieste, affording him his first opportunity to embark upon biological research. His first scientific problem was assigned to him by his professor, Claus, and it proved a challenging one, indeed. Since ancient times—as Aristotle had noted in his writings—scientists had been unable to delineate the precise location of the sex glands of the male eel. A hypothesis concerning the question had been advanced by Syrski to the effect that a lobular organ of the eel, a structure of undetermined function, might in fact be the "missing" male sex gland. Freud proceeded in his work to check this hypothesis with the energetic and concentrated application which thenceforth was to characterize his scientific work. In pursuit of the problem, Freud dissected and analyzed several hundred specimens, bringing his researches to a successful conclusion by establishing the correctness of the hypothesis that the lobular organ of the eel actually was the testes. He added the suggestion that the lobular organ could develop into either a male or female sex gland. Jones observed that it was a poetic touch for the future discoverer of the castration complex to begin his career in research by establishing the existence of a male sex gland. Freud, however, was far from satisfied with the result of his first investigation and also with the guidance of his first scientific mentor.

The outstanding biological research laboratory in Vienna at the time was the Physiological Institute headed by Brücke. It was to his laboratory that Freud arranged to be transferred. Brücke was a colleague and follower of Helmholtz, part of a group of rising biologists who had united in opposition to the "vitalist" theory of their teacher, J. Müller. Their main orientation was to explain biological phenomena in terms of physics and chemistry. According to Freud, Brücke influenced him more than any other professional teacher and, in fact, it took Freud many years and his own analysis before he could free himself from the narrow physicalist approach to the phenomena of the mind in favor of a more dynamic psychological outlook.

Brücke set Freud to work on a study of the embryological origin of the nerve roots of a low form of spinal animal—petromyzon. The preliminary report of this study appeared in 1877. His second report on the subject was amazingly complete and thorough—eighty-six pages in length. In it, Freud made a major discovery demonstrating the evolutionary continuity of the structural elements of the cells of the central nervous system from lower to higher animals. Thus, from the field of comparative anatomy and embryology, Freud contributed another link in the chain of evidence substantiating Darwin's theory of evolution, a theory which was the subject of wide debate at the time. It was in Brücke's laboratory, too, that Freud met Breuer. It was the beginning of an association which was to prove so momentous in both their lives and in the history of psychoanalysis.

Freud's next paper, concerning the construction of nerve fibers and nerve cells in the crayfish, appeared in 1882. The work required special microscopic technique at which Freud was becoming increasingly adept. Like its predecessor, this paper dealt with the histological elements of the central nervous system. Freud was the first to demonstrate that the axis cylinders of nerve fibers are fibrillary in nature. In discussing his findings and related reflections on the subject, Freud put forth his concepts of the anatomy and the functioning of the units of the nervous system. Although his views were never widely publicized, he had in fact anticipated what was subsequently a major development of neurophysiology and neuroanatomy, namely, the concept of the neurone theory. Jeliffe, Brun and other authorities feel that Freud should be ranked along with His, Forel, Cajal and Waldeyer as one of the enunciators of the neurone theory.

It was in his fourth contribution to biological science, however, that Freud indirectly served as one of the immortal benefactors of mankind and came close, while still a young man, to realizing his burning desire for everlasting fame. In a masterfully comprehensive study of the properties of coca, Freud suggested that the topical anesthetic qualities of the alkaloid, cocaine, deserved further investigation. While away on a visit to his betrothed, the decisive experimental work which established the usefulness of cocaine as a local anesthetic in the practice of surgery was done by a friend and colleague of Freud's, Koller, with whose name this discovery has been linked. Freud's primary interest was in the general constitutional effects of the coca leaf and not in the ability of the extract to assuage local pain. Jones suggests that it is doubtful whether Freud, a relative stranger to the practice of surgery, would have conceived the precise application of cocaine which Koller had. In any event, Freud's thoroughness, enthusiasm and imaginativeness in the study of coca clearly laid the basis for Koller's discovery.

Later observers in the field of biology, upon reviewing Freud's work, felt that the imaginative quality and thoroughness of his biological researches were so impressive that biology had lost one of its potentially great contributors when Freud turned his attention to psychology.

# 2.

# *Freud as a Neurologist*

It was Brücke, Freud's teacher, who urged him to consider a method for making a living and accordingly advised Freud to complete the study of medicine. Freud did so reluctantly, but carried into this new field the same passionate urge for investigation that had characterized his early, brilliant promise as a biologist. Freud's meticulous histological investigations brought him to the attention of his professor, Meynert, at the Cerebral Anatomy Institute. For a while it appeared that Freud was being prepared to take over some of Meynert's responsibilities. In his autobiography Freud joked about the wild diagnoses he made in his clinical demonstrations to American students, but he was nevertheless proud to be the first doctor in Vienna to make an ante-mortem diagnosis of peripheral neuritis which was subsequently confirmed at autopsy.

In all, Freud published over twenty papers and encyclopedia articles in neurology and neuropathology. Freud's interest and contributions ranged over all areas of the field. He wrote on histological technique, microanatomy, pathological malformations, clinical descriptions and general conceptualizations of neurology. He was regarded as one of the oustanding experts on the microanatomy of the medulla oblongata and the recognized European authority on cerebral paralysis in children.

A sampling of only a few of Freud's contributions to the field of neurology demonstrates his mastery of the field. In 1884 Freud published in the English journal, *Brain,* "A New Histological Method for the Study of Nerve Tracts in the Brain and Spinal Chord." It was a method which he had devised himself. More meticulous and painstaking, however, was Freud's microanatomical study of the medulla oblongata. In a series of studies which required many hours of studious application to the microscope, Freud carefully established the anatomical connection of the sensory tracts, the interolivary tracts, the acoustic nuclei and the various peduncles of the brain. From the clinical point of view he reported carefully studied cases of cerebral hemorrhage, congenital ataxias and deformities, and a case of syringomyelia, a neurological entity which was rarely diagnosed in those days.

But his mastery of the field of neurology was demonstrated in two additional fields, namely, the cerebral paralyses of children and aphasia. On his way back from studying with Charcot at the Salpêtrière, Freud paused briefly in Berlin for further training in the neurological disorders of children. This was in preparation for a post as chief of the neurological service of a children's institute in Vienna. For many years he was chief neurologist to this service, and from this experience together with his friend, the pediatrician, Dr. Rie, he wrote a definitive monograph on one-sided cerebral paralysis in children in 1891. This was a detailed clinical study of thirty-five cases under their personal observation. A further study which Freud wrote alone appeared in 1893 under the title, "Cerebral Diplegia in Children." Charcot's successor, Pierre Marie, said of the study, "This monograph is unquestionably the most complete, the most accurate and thoughtful which has yet appeared on the confusing problem of cerebral diplegia of infancy about which so little is known." From clinical and pathological investigation Freud concluded that many of the so-called birth traumas actually were misnomers, the conditions having existed in the infant or foetus before the experience of parturition. Nothnagel, a leading medical authority who was preparing an encyclopedia, called upon Freud to write the definitive article on the cerebral paralyses of children, thus giving concrete evidence to the authoritative position which Freud held in the field. Of all of his neurological contributions those dealing with the cerebral paralyses of children received widest recognition and remembrance in neurological circles.

Freud's monograph on aphasia which appeared in 1891 was one of his favorites and, in more recent years, it has come to be regarded as one of the classic studies of modern neurology. In it Freud was one of the first to appreciate the implications of Hughlings Jackson's evolutionary concept of the functioning of the central nervous system. Perhaps the leading authority on aphasia today, Kurt Goldstein, has indicated his indebtedness to the holistic, dynamic and genetic approach which Freud used in the study of aphasia. Because of these qualities in the work Bernfeld regards Freud's study, *On Aphasia,* as the first "Freudian" work. In it Freud maintained that the localization of speech function to definite, concrete, minute centers had been overly emphasized. He stressed the importance of the dynamic interplay of functions from different dynamic centers of mental activity utilizing the genetic functional levels which Jackson had introduced. In this work Freud also coined the term, "agnosia"; the concept connected with it has become a standard conceptual tool in the modern-day study of aphasia.

The latter part of Freud's brilliant career as a neurologist fell under the shadow of his growing interest in the psychology of neurosis. In May, 1894, he wrote to Fliess, ". . . . I am pretty well alone here in tackling the neuroses. They regard me rather as a monomaniac, while I have the distinct feeling that I have touched on one of the great secrets of nature. There is something comic about the incongruity between one's own and other people's estimate of one's work. Look at my book on the diplegias which I knocked together almost casually with a minimum of interest and effort. It has been a huge success. The critics say the nicest things about it and the French reviews in particular are full of praise. . . . But for the really good things like the 'Aphasia,' the 'Obsessional Ideas' which threaten to appear shortly, and the coming 'Etiology and Theory of the Neuroses' I can expect no more than a respectable flop. This is bewildering and somewhat embittering."

# 3.

# *Freud as a Translator*

*"He had a very considerable gift for language of which
his becoming later a recognized master of German prose
was only one example. Besides being completely at home
in Latin and Greek he acquired a thorough knowledge
of French and English; in addition, he taught himself
Italian and Spanish. He had, of course, been taught
Hebrew. He was especially fond of English and . . . .
for ten years he read nothing but English books."*
—ERNEST JONES, THE LIFE AND WORK OF SIGMUND FREUD

As a schoolboy he kept a diary in Greek. In his
introduction to the Hebrew version of *Totem and
Taboo* Freud regretted that he did not know
Hebrew or at least that he was not conversant
with the language of the Holy Writ. Of the
English writers he was especially partial to Shake-
speare, Galsworthy and Shaw. He made brilliant
use of his knowledge of philology and linguistics
in his *Interpretation of Dreams,* and independently
came upon the concept of the antithetical sense of
primal words.

In 1880, at the request of Theodor Gomperz, a
prominent philosopher and historian of Vienna,

Freud translated several philosophical essays of John Stuart Mill from English into German. Freud minimized whatever philosophical tendencies there were in him, but this was true only in a formal sense. While he was not interested in specific systems or schools of philosophy as such, his scientific conceptualization was of the highest philosophical order, and he strove for the broadest possible integration of data in a meaningful frame of reference. Freud does not seem to have been particularly sympathetic with many of Mill's philosophical views, especially those on the emancipation of women. He was, however, appreciative of the treatment accorded Plato from whom he borrowed many suggestions concerning the function of memory. Jokingly Freud often said that whatever he knew of philosophy he derived from his experience of having translated the essays of John Stuart Mill.

As a translator, Freud's main contribution to science is associated with his bringing to the German-speaking medical world the works of Charcot and Bernheim on neurology, hypnotism and suggestion. Freud was a translator in more senses than one; in lectures, case reports and articles as well, he transmitted the views of the French schools of Salpêtrière and Nancy to the academies of Vienna. To understand his role one must appreciate how different French neurology of the day was from the German, especially as regards the problem of hysteria. The views of the French were not only at odds with those of the Germans but were held in suspicion above all in Vienna. Through the use of hypnosis, Charcot had been able to establish that the symptoms of hysterics were genuine; the patients were not theatrical malingerers; men as well as women could suffer from hysteria. His school in Paris had become a center both for the teaching of neurology and for research in hysteria from the functional point of view. Viennese neurology was still steeped in the concept of anatomical localization. Freud's own professor, Meynert, had advanced a theory which ascribed the cause of hysterical and other symptoms to cricumscribed circulatory disturbances in the brain. As far as hysteria was concerned the two great medical centers of Europe were worlds apart, and it was Freud who in effect assumed the role of trying to bring these two worlds together.

Upon completing his medical studies, Freud received a traveling scholarship to study in Paris where, as he later said, he fell under the spell of the great Charcot. He requested and obtained permission to translate from French into German Charcot's *New Lectures on Diseases of the Nervous System, Especially Hysteria*. Freud credited Charcot in part with the idea of the importance of sexuality in the etiology of hysteria. He tried to interest Charcot in Breuer's cathartic method of treating hysteria, but apparently this information fell on uninterested ears. In 1892 Freud translated

Charcot's famous *Leçons du Mardi à la Salpêtrière*. Freud was more than a translator of this work. He wrote an introduction describing the difference between the French and German approaches to neuropathology and embellished his translation with a large number of footnotes, some of which were elucidations of the text, others constituting critical objections and marginal observations. Kris points out that Freud appeared to have failed to obtain Charcot's permission to do this, and in "The Psychopathology of Everyday Life" Freud conjectured that the author "must have been dissatisfied with this arbitrary behavior."

The school of Nancy, headed by Bernheim and Liébault, had a much more dynamic and psychological approach to the problem of hysteria than did the school at Salpêtrière. While Charcot felt that hysterical symptoms were genuine but related to functional dissociation due to some hereditary weakness of the hysterics' nervous system, Bernheim emphasized the role of suggestion in both the formation and cure of hysterical symptoms. In his book *New Studies on Hypnotism, Suggestion and Psychotherapy* which Freud translated into German, Bernheim demonstrated how the therapeutic effect of hypnotism in the treatment of hysteria could be ascribed to the power of suggestion. He had advanced the psychological approach to the problem of hysteria one step further.

There were two subsequent occasions in his life

when Freud set his hand again to the task of translation, but these efforts were by no means as ambitious as the fundamental works of Charcot and Bernheim. In 1926 Anna Freud arranged the German edition of Dr. Israel Levine's book, entitled *The Unconscious*. This book, written in English, dealt with the influence of the unconscious in literary creations. It included a short essay on the great English writer, Samuel Butler, which Freud translated into German. The circumstances under which Freud translated the charming animal story *Topsy* by Marie Bonaparte were much more dramatic. In 1938, while awaiting permission from the Nazis to leave Austria, Freud and his daughter, Anna, translated the story of a chow dog from French. While they were busy at their task of translation, Marie Bonaparte was successfully occupied in securing Freud's release from the Germans.

# 4.

# *The Interpretation of*
# *Dreams*

*"He solved the dark enigma and was a man most mighty."*

*The Interpretation of Dreams* occupies a unique and special position in Freud's life and in the history of psychoanalysis. Writing a preface to the Third Revised English Edition in 1931, Freud stated, "It contains, even according to my present-day judgement, the most valuable of all the discoveries it has been my good fortune to make. Insight such as this falls to one's lot but once in a lifetime."

This book is in effect a partial record of his own psychoanalysis begun in the year following his father's death in 1896. Freud cured himself of a number of neurotic symptoms by systematic self-observation, of which the analysis of his own dreams was one of the most important elements. Dream interpretation was a field in which he felt his complete sense of mastery. When he realized the serious error into which he had fallen in connection with his "seduction" theory of the etiology of the neuroses, he was sustained by his faith in the solid scientific basis of dream interpretation. By general consensus *The Interpretation of Dreams* is regarded as Freud's most original and creative work. The publication of this book in 1900 (actually 1899) marks one of the revolutionary turning points in the history of man's knowledge of his own mind.

*The Interpretation of Dreams* grew out of Freud's study of the neuroses and marked a culminating point in their investigation. Dreaming, a universally intriguing experience, whose significance had eluded countless generations—Freud placed within the continuum of man's psychological experience. He did so by applying to mental life the concept of causality which scientists assume in their investigation of the physical world. This principle of psychic determinism, the conviction that mental phenomena have a cause, enabled Freud to demonstrate that dreams could be interpreted, that they had a meaning which could be unraveled in a systematic way. The idea that dreams could be understood occurred to Freud when he observed how regularly they emerged in the associations of patients whose symptoms he was striving to understand. The structure of dreams and the structure of symptoms, he discovered, were identical; they were both compromise formations, the resultant of the

[ 23 ]

interplay of conflicting forces in the mind. An impulse, usually from childhood, of which the individual was unaware, seeks discharge and is opposed by the activity of another agency of the mind. It was the mutual effect of these contesting forces in the mind which brought about the disguises and distortions which made dreams and symptoms equally unintelligible.

But there was also an economy to dreaming. Dreams serve the function of protecting sleep from disturbances of whatever origin by offering the sleeper in a distorted, hallucinatory fashion the fulfillment of an infantile wish—infantile, because the genetic approach which Breuer and Freud had introduced so effectively in the *Studies in Hysteria* had demonstrated to Freud that the wish behind the dream, like the wish contained in the hysterical symptom, could be—in fact, had to be—traced back to the earliest years of life.

The plan of the book was carefully laid out by the author. Skilled therapist that he was, Freud proceeded cautiously with his reader—presenting first what was superficial, acceptable and credible, then proceeding in easy steps to the depths which harbored so much that was new and shocking. It was well toward the middle of *The Interpretation Dreams* that Freud first described to the world the existence of the oedipus complex, perhaps the most striking of his many ideas which were destined "to disturb the sleep of the world." The discovery of

THE INTERPRETATION OF DREAMS

the oedipus complex was of greatest moment in the development of Freud's thoughts. It removed many of the roadblocks barring the way to the solution of such problems as infantile sexuality and the phenomena of transference.

The strict determinism of Freud's method of dream interpretation led him into fields whose connection with the original problems of his investigations could hardly have been surmised. Hints of insight into the psychology of religion, art, character formation, mythology, wit and literature are adumbrated in this book. Freud considered the study of dreams "the royal road to the unconscious," and in the ten years which followed the publication of this book Freud devoted himself in a large measure to amplifying, expanding, and driving to a logical conclusion, the hints and suggestions contained therein. The basic working concepts which dominated Freud's thinking in that period were psychic determinism, unconscious conflict, and the oedipus conflict. The pursuit of these ideas led inevitably to the next group of major contributions—*The Psychopathology of Everyday Life, Jokes and Their Relation to the Unconscious, Three Contributions to the Theory of Sexuality,* and somewhat later to *Totem and Taboo.*

From the sales point of view, *The Interpretation of Dreams* was far from a success. The first edition of the book comprised 600 copies. According to the records of Freud's publisher, Franz Deuticke, it required eight years to sell these copies. In the first six weeks 123 were sold and in the next two years only 228 more. Jones points out that Freud was paid the equivalent of $209.00 for the book. There were, however, eight editions of the book in Freud's lifetime. A shortened version of the book which Freud had prepared, entitled *On Dreams,* did, however, become in later years one of the most popular of Freud's publications. Most striking of all, however, is the fact that this fundamental work proved so comprehensive and thorough that hardly any fundamental revisions were required in subsequent editions. The book has remained a rich source of ideas for further research by other analysts and in some cases a short sentence or a footnote has been used as the basis for founding a deviant school of psychoanalysis.

# 5.

# *The Theory of Drives*

Freud's psychoanalytic thoughts developed in an integrated fashion because he was constantly at work correlating the data of his observational experience with the body of his theory. Accordingly, only for convenience of presentation, have his contributions to psychoanalysis proper been subsumed in this essay under the headings "The Theory of Drives," "Psychological Theory" and "Contributions to Therapy."

Fundamental in Freud's thinking was the idea of mental activity as a manifestation of work done, of energy expended in some form or other. Strictly speaking, he thought of an interplay of forces, for throughout his writings Freud was dualistic in his approach; he envisaged the operation of the mind as a form of dynamic equilibrium between opposing forces, an equilibrium which was constantly being disturbed and re-established. As this section will demonstrate, his concept of what constituted the energizing forces of the mind went through many stages of development and change.

Freud credited the beginning of psychoanalysis to Breuer's investigation of hysteria by means of hypnosis. This method consisted of inducing hypnotic recollection of the "traumatic" events. When the patient relived the painful experience under hypnosis and gave full expression to the associated emotions the symptoms of hysteria disappeared. The patient was said to have "abreacted" the associated undischarged affect, and the principle of therapy was referred to as "catharsis." The symptoms of the illness could be traced to the effects of a memory which, although forgotten, continued nevertheless in a dynamic way to influence the life of the patient. For the first time in the history of psychology the concept of a dynamic unconscious had been introduced. By connecting the phenomena of mental illness to the events in the patient's past experience and by indicating the need to trace these events as far back as possible in the life history of the individual, Breuer and Freud enunciated what was to become one of the fundamentals of psychoanalytic theory and practice—the genetic approach to mental phenomena.

The *Studies in Hysteria,* by Breuer and Freud, which appeared in 1895 were written at the insistence of Freud. He contributed four of the five case histories and wrote the section on therapy. The conceptual model which the authors used was that of a foreign body imbedded in the matrix of the tissues, a concept close to their interest in histology and pathology. The repressed memory, the secret foreign body in the psyche, grew by accretion—drawing into its structure thoughts and memories associated to it by contiguity, contrast, etc. The precise form of the energy by which this memory was activated and by which in turn it activated other mental constructs was not clear in the minds of the authors. They referred to it variously as affect, emotion, and excitation. Fundamentally, they thought of it as related to a sum of excitation in the central nervous system which had available alternative pathways of discharge. If denied release in the life of the mind, this sum of excitation might innervate somatic nerve pathways giving rise to hysterical symptoms through a process for which Freud coined the term "conversion."

Even before the *Studies in Hysteria* appeared in print the views of Breuer and Freud began to diverge sharply. Clinical data impressed Freud more and more with the idea that the trauma in hysteria was invariably a sexual one and that the motives for repression were defensive, i.e., psychological ones. Breuer, on the other hand, emphasized the etiological significance of the hypnoid state for hysteria. Memories, he maintained, were repressed not because they were extruded from consciousness by virtue of their painful nature but, on the contrary, because they had been introduced into the mind of the patient at a time of disturbed consciousness, namely, the hypnoid state. The hypnoid state, in turn, was a physiological functional disturbance of the mind based upon the congenital dissociative tendency of the hysteric.

Freud expanded his views of the function of defense in hysteria to include the obsessional neuroses as well, and in 1894 he included both these clinical entities under the heading of a paper entitled "The Defence Neuro-Psychoses." The last paragraph of this paper is memorable because in it he elucidated the important working concept of "cathexis"—a concept which was basic in all his subsequent work. In this paragraph he states, "I should like finally to dwell for a moment on the hypothesis I have made use of in the exposition of the defence neuroses. I mean the conception that among the psychic functions there is something which should be differentiated (an amount of affect, a sum of excitation), something having all the attributes of a quantity— although we possess no means of measuring it—a something which is capable of increase, decrease, displacement and discharge, and which extends itself over the memory-traces of an idea like an electric charge over the surface of the body. We can apply this hypothesis, which by the way already underlies our theory of 'abreaction,' in the same sense as the physicist employs the conception of a fluid electric current. For the present it is justified by its utility in correlating and explaining diverse psychical conditions."

[ 30 ]

The libido theory, as one can see, had its precursor here although at the time Freud had not yet discovered the oedipus complex or infantile sexuality. In the absence of a theory of infantile sexuality, this makes comprehensible Freud's famous "error" of the seduction theory in which he tried to account for the childhood sexual manifestations of patients with hysteria by assuming that in each case there had occurred some actual seduction of the child by an adult. And if it were not for Freud's self-analysis and his discovery of the oedipus complex, man's knowledge of the hidden depths of his mind might have been arrested at this point.

In addition to the implications for sexual theory discussed in the section on "The Interpretation of Dreams" the substitutive expression of sexual wishes in terms of oral and anal images inexorably led Freud to a novel and broadened understanding of sexuality in human life. If *The Interpretation of Dreams* occasioned derision, the publication of the *Three Essays on the Theory of Sexuality* in 1905 provoked outraged opprobrium. The notion of infantile sexuality was offensive to the officially established morality of the day, although Freud remarked that it was a discovery any nursemaid could have made. According to Strachey, "Freud's 'Three Essays on the Theory of Sexuality' stand, there can be no doubt, beside his 'Interpretation of Dreams' as his most momentous and original contributions to human knowledge."

The ideas contained in the *Three Essays* opened to Freud the widest vista for correlating biology and psychology. He had, indeed, come upon one of the great secrets of nature. Sexuality was present at birth; it followed a biologically predetermined pattern of maturation; it was vested in the zones and functioning of the body; until the final stamp of its constitution was imprinted in the later years of puberty, sexuality was capable of the widest developmental variation as a result of environmental influence. The symptoms of the neurotic and the aberrations of the pervert, the sex life of the adult and the development of the child; the impulses of the dream and the fantasies of literature—all could be encompassed within one frame of reference. But, above all, sexuality was a force capable "of increase, decrease, displacement and discharge." It answered in all respects Freud's requirement for a more precise energizing force in mental activity.

The transition to the libido theory was a quick and natural step. In keeping with his dualistic approach Freud now conceived of mental activity as representative of two sets of drives—libidinal drives seeking gratification and ultimately related to the preservation of the species were opposed by the ego drives seeking to preserve the existence of the individual by curbing, when necessary, the dangerous (antisocial) sexual wishes. The operation of the libidinal drives was, for the most part, un-

conscious and corresponded in its behavior to those
qualities of the psychic apparatus which Freud
had designated as the system Ucs. Since the work-
ings of the ego drives seemed at this stage to be
self-evident, Freud concentrated his analytic efforts
primarily on the manifold variations of the libido.
His speculations concerning the libido theory were
founded on biochemical formulations, which in-
cidentally proved remarkably apt for an individual
working in a period when endocrinology was in its
very infancy.

As Freud expanded his therapeutic efforts from
the realm of neurosis into that of psychosis, he
encountered psychopathological formations which
could not be correlated adequately within his theoretical framework of libidinal versus self-preserva-
tive drives. To account for such phenomena as
hypochondriasis, megalomania, delusion formation
and withdrawal from the world of reality, a modi-
fication of the libido theory became necessary.
Freud proposed to distinguish between the libidinal
cathexes of representations of the self as opposed to
libidinal cathexes of representations of objects of
the external world. To the former he gave the name
of narcissism. The psychopathological formations of
the psychoses enumerated above could be understood from this point of view as representing
surplus investments of libido in the self. Accordingly, he distinguished the psychoses which he
called "narcissistic neuroses" from the psychoneu-

roses which he titled "transference neuroses." The concept of narcissism which was introduced in 1914 in a paper entitled "On Narcissism: An Introduction" also proved useful in understanding such normally abnormal forms of irrationality as falling in love and pride in one's own children. It also afforded new insight into such phenomena as sleep which could be regarded as a special form of narcissistic regression, and group formation in which the image of the leader of the group was invested with narcissistic cathexis.

The concept of narcissism, however, resolved only a few of the difficulties inherent in the theory of drives. Freud had assumed that the accumulation of undischarged libido resulted in a state of painful tension while the discharge of libido was accompanied by feelings of pleasure. It seemed a self-evident biological principal that the organism operates in such a way as to seek pleasure and avoid unpleasure or pain. But the manifestations of the role of aggression in the mental life of man, especially the phenomena of masochism, presented Freud with a new series of problems which required solution. His growing clinical experience brought to light phenomena which could not be integrated into his working body of theory. Among these clinical entities were the perverse beating fantasies of the masochist, the negative therapeutic reaction, the character type of the exception who elaborated his childhood misfortune to his perpetual self-injury, individuals who perpetrated crimes in order to seek punishment to alleviate a sense of guilt, or the sad experience of those wrecked by the very achievement of success. But above all, it was the intrusion of aggression into the sexual life of the individual which proved most baffling. This could be observed with special clarity in the ambivalent attitude of the melancholiac toward the lost love object and in the hostile attitude of certain women toward their lovers.

How were these phenomena to be reconciled with the pleasure principle in the ego-libido theory? During the "metapsychological period" (1915-1920) Freud grappled with this question in various publications. In "The Instincts and Their Vicissitudes" (1915), in conformity with the pleasure-pain principle, he attempted to understand masochistic phenomena as vicissitudes of the sadistic component of the libido. The essential mechanism in masochism, he felt, was the interchange of passive for active instinctual aims and the substitution of the object for the subject. This was a period of transition and Freud was only tentatively satisfied with his results. Speaking of the derivation of masochism from sadism through the various instinctual vicissitudes, he wrote, "Whether there is besides this a more direct masochistic satisfaction is highly doubtful. A primary masochism not derived in the manner I have described from sadism does not appear to be met with." Yet in a famous footnote which he added to this paper nine years later he wrote, "In later works relating to problems of instinctual life, I have expressed the opposite view." Freud, it would appear, was now on the verge of a major reorientation of his theory of the mental life of man.

This major reorientation took place in 1920 in his essay, *Beyond the Pleasure Principle*. In a bold departure from his previous theories Freud extended his dualistic concept of human drives by putting forward the notion of two types of instincts, libido and aggression, both derived in turn from broader, all-pervading biological principles— an instinct of love (Eros) and an instinct toward death and destruction (Thanatos). His speculations took him beyond the limitations of direct clinical observation and he was correct in surmising that many of his followers would not take the leap with him. These two drives, Eros and Thanatos, he maintained, operate in different ways in the human psyche, never in total isolation. They make themselves manifest concretely in a particular psychological activity in various degrees of combination or fusion. Directed toward the external world of objects, primary aggression becomes the instinct of destruction . . . the wish to power. Fused with libido in the service of the sexual instinct it becomes true sadism. Bound libidinally within the self it becomes the original basic erotogenic masochism. Freud's theorizing about the nature of

[ 36 ]

man's mental life had led him to a theory of life itself. The introduction of the concept of a death instinct evoked a stormy controversy within psycho-analytic circles, a controversy which has not yet subsided.

The new dual instinct theory of libido versus aggression dispensed with the oppositional role of the ego drives. The function of self-preservation (the ego drives) which formerly had operated in opposition to the libido now required re-examination, and the problem of its position in mental life presaged Freud's subsequent formulation of the structural hypothesis of the psychic apparatus.

# 6.

# *Psychological Theory*

". . . . a man like me cannot live without a hobby-horse, a consuming passion—in Schiller's words a tyrant. I have found my tyrant, and in his service I know no limits. My tyrant is psychology; it has always been my distant, beckoning goal and now, since I have hit on the neuroses, it has come so much the nearer. I am plagued with two ambitions: to see how the theory of mental functioning takes shape if quantitative considerations, a sort of economics of nerve-force, are introduced into it; and secondly, to extract from psychopathology what may be of benefit to normal psychology. Actually a satisfactory general theory of neuropsychotic disturbances is impossible if it cannot be brought into association with clear assumptions about normal mental processes."

—LETTER TO W. FLIESS, DATED MAY 25, 1895

To this beckoning goal of a comprehensive general theory of psychology Freud remained devoted the rest of his life. As his understanding and clinical experience grew, Freud kept re-examining and revising the frame of reference of his theory. In this section are included excerpts from various periods reflecting the changing stages in the development of Freud's general psychological conceptions.

[ 38 ]

True to his early training in biology and neurology, Freud made tentative efforts to conceptualize mental functioning in terms of the anatomy and physiology of the nervous system. In the main the physiology followed the fundamental formulations of Helmholtz, Fechner and others, authorities who stressed the importance of energy conceptions in biological and psychological phenomena. In 1895 Freud prepared "A Project for a Scientific Psychology" which he never published. This "Project" was later found among his letters to Fliess. In this work he tried to ascribe mental functioning to specific sets of neurones operating in such a way as to keep constant within the central nervous system a state of excitation. Changes in the level and quality of mental functioning were interpreted as reflections of shifts in the quantitative charge of energy available to different organizations of neurones. Freud himself apparently did not prize this conceptualization very highly for he made no attempt to retrieve the "Project" or to publish it.

Probably as a result of his self-analysis, Freud was able to abandon his strict adherence to concepts borrowed from neurophysiology and physics in favor of more dynamic psychological thinking. In the famous chapter VII of *The Interpretation of Dreams* (1900) Freud attempted to elaborate, for the first time, a theory of the human mind in psychological terms alone. Using as his starting point the fact that the dream was a visual hallucinatory experience, Freud tried to conceptualize the functioning of the mind in terms of a compound optical instrument which would at the same time take into account the elements of psychic determinism, unconscious conflict and infantile wishes. He visualized the human psychic apparatus as operating on three different functional levels or "systems" — Perception-Consciousness, Preconscious, and Unconscious. Each system was endowed with characteristic qualities and demonstrated above all different methods or degrees of binding psychic excitation. The psychic excitation traveled in a certain direction from perception to discharge, usually in the form of some motor activity. The unconscious was the source or reservoir of the excitation. In it the energy of excitation was highly mobile and displaceable. By attaching itself to elements of the preconscious, which was in the main composed of elements of memory readily available to consciousness through the application of the function of attention, an unconscious wish could become manifest through a set of preconscious derivatives. The greater the quantity of excitation the more numerous and vivid were the derivatives of the unconscious wish. Because of the special conditions operating in the state of sleep a regressive direction of the discharge of excitation becomes possible. In the mind of the immobilized sleeper an unconscious wish may travel not in the direction from perception toward motor discharge but contrariwise, i.e., regressively *toward* perception, resulting in a visual hallucination, a dream. Although formulated for the specific task of explaining the phenomena of dreaming, these dynamic concepts of Freud had the widest possible application for a general theory of mental functioning.

Freud demonstrated this very conclusively in his next major publication on the subject in 1904—*The Psychopathology of Everyday Life*. He showed how the principles of psychic determinism and unconscious conflict had a general validity and applicability beyond the confines of dreams and neurosis. In fact, the three psychic systems which he had postulated in *The Interpretation of Dreams*— Ppt-Cs, Pcs, Ucs—corresponded to his clinical experience in trying to make the unconscious conscious. From the point of view of the patient, the motives of certain actions were conscious at the time of their commission. In other cases, with the expenditure of some effort, especially the application of attention, the intentions of the action were readily amenable to consciousness; the intention behind such actions may be considered preconscious. In still other cases a considerable amount of work had to be done before the patient could come to see what was the probable intention of his action. The intention in such cases Freud described as unconscious. In *The Psychopathology of Everyday Life* Freud indicated that many of the events of daily life, like slips of the tongue and pen, the forgetting of names, the misplacing of objects, jokes, puns, etc., were meaningful and could be approached in a scientific manner through psychoanalysis. Parapraxes, as he calls these actions, were compromise formations, derivatives of the break-through of a repressed intention which use many of the mechanisms recognizable in the structure of dreams and symptoms. A general theory of mental functioning based upon the conceptual framework of psychoanalysis was beginning to emerge.

In 1915 Freud projected a series of twelve essays which were to synthesize his psychological conceptions under the heading of "Metapsychology." By this term he meant "describing a mental process in all its aspects, dynamic, topographic, and economic," i.e., an understanding of the interplay of the energies involved, the part of the psychic apparatus concerned, and the shifts of quantities of energy which take place. This represented an attempt on Freud's part to expand his concepts beyond the model of the psychic apparatus as outlined in *The Interpretation of Dreams*. A more precise structural framework had to be created to account for the various formations resulting from the struggle between the ego and libido drives. Using the metapsychological approach, he hoped to achieve better definitions of the phenomena of the psychoses, dreams, and the perversions.

The twelve essays which Freud projected were written within the space of a few months, but unfortunately only five of the essays were published and have survived. Of these the essay, "The Unconscious," is considered the outstanding. It was the most comprehensive theoretical exposition after *The Interpretation of Dreams* combining general philosophical and psychological considerations with Freud's more recently acquired insight into psychopathology as a result of his widening clinical experience. The "metapsychological period" was a transitional phase between Freud's conception of the psyche as portrayed in the Dream book and his later conception of the "structural hypothesis" of the psyche.

Freud's revision of the theory of drives in 1920 had immediate and far-reaching consequences for the framework of his psychological theory. The tripartite metapsychological analysis of mental phenomena according to the economic, topographic, and dynamic point of view was extended and, in fact, supplanted by an entirely new conceptualization. There were many reasons for this change. To begin with, by introducing the duality of libido versus aggression, the role of the ego drives as the deterring, modifying influences on the libido was eliminated. The fact remained, however, that there were indeed many functions which previously had been grouped as representatives of the ego drives. To what part of the psyche were they now to be assigned? Clinical experience had shown that some of these functions operated consciously while others were carried out quite unconsciously. Notable among the latter is the resistance which is encountered in the course of psychoanalytic practice. A patient accepts the task of pursuing a line of thought freely, but his associations fail as he appears to be getting closer to what has been repressed. The dynamic effect of this resistance can be made known to the patient by an interpretation, but the resistance per se remains unconscious. The patient does not know what it is or how to describe it. Here, said Freud, is something in the ego which is nonetheless unconscious, which behaves very much like repressed memories, which continues to influence conscious behavior, and which requires special work before it can be made conscious.

There were, furthermore, other clinical manifestations of a functional split in the psyche. Many of these were related to the activity of the recently emphasized aggressive drives. Such, for example, was the situation in moral masochism and melancholia, in which one part of the psyche seems to inflict pain and suffering upon another part. To compound perplexity, a persistent need for punishment observed in the life history of many patients seemed to indicate an attitude of guilt of which the individual was quite unaware. In short, not only were the evil, antisocial impulses in man established mainly in the unconscious, but the working of a great portion of human morality seemed to be relegated with equal foundation to an area beyond the ken of consciousness. A system of conceptualization which assigned domicile in the unconscious exclusively to the repressed instinctual drives was no longer tenable.

Freud took note of these considerations in an epoch-making book, *The Ego and the Id* (1923), in which he reformulated his theories in terms of a structural organization of the mind, a grouping of mental activities into three major *functional* centers, the ego, the id, and the superego. This view has since been referred to as the structural hypothesis of the psychic apparatus. But it must be emphasized that these subdivisions are operational concepts rather than immutably demarcated compartments. Intrapsychic conflict is the situation *par excellence* which lays bare the differentiation of these functional centers in the mind.

Broadly speaking, the ego is that group of functions which orients the individual toward the external world; receives, interprets and organizes stimuli from whatever source; acts as the executant for the drives and correlates these demands of the instincts with a proper regard for the superego and the world of reality. It is through the study of the activities of the ego that knowledge of the other two psychic agencies may be obtained. The id (a third person, almost alien appellation) is the reservoir of the instincts and the recipient of what has been repressed. The superego is a "split-off" portion of the ego, a residue of the early history of the individual's moral training, a precipitate of his most important childhood identifications. By virtue of its critical function of observing the self as it were "from above" it derives its name, the superego. Other associated functions are centered in this structure. The concept of the ideal image toward which the individual aspires is one example.

The relationship of these agencies to the quality of consciousness deserves special note, for it is this which distinguishes this new hypothesis from Freud's previous theories. In this delineation, consciousness and unconsciousness are used in a descriptive, qualitative sense alone, no longer in the sense of a special system of the mind. The id is said to be unconscious. But, whereas some of the activities of the ego and superego are conscious, others are unconscious.

This essay cannot contain the limits and details of the structural hypothesis. In fact, Freud sketched out only the broadest outlines of this concept, leaving it to further studies to amplify and implement his ideas. The structural hypothesis, however, has had the most far-reaching implications for psychoanalytic practice and research. It has proved so cogent and practical a formulation that Jones was led to declare, "How did we ever get along without it!" Freud, however, true to his searching spirit and integrating mind, continued to dwell on many of the problems which his new theory of drives and the psychic apparatus posed to a general psychoanalytic psychology. At the time of his death in 1939, he was at work on an outline of psycho-analysis in which he undertook to clarify and define his theories. Thus, to the end he remained devoted to his "tyrant"—a general theory of psychology, a theory which he continued to change as his knowledge and understanding of the human mind grew.

# 7.

## *Contributions to Therapy*

THERE can be no question but that Freud takes his place in history as one of the great liberators of the mentally ill. By insisting that the symptoms and the verbal productions of neurotics and psychotics had a meaning, a significance that could be comprehended, he served to dispel a deeply rooted prejudice directed against a very considerable segment of humanity. This prejudice, entertained inside as well as outside of the medical profession, had served to stigmatize neurotic patients and to place them rather beyond the pale of professional sympathy. As a result of Freud's teachings it has become proper to listen to patients, all patients, in a way that had not been done before. In his investigation of his patients, Freud eschewed any notion of condemnation or stigmatization. Above all, he felt the therapist should respect the patient's integrity and should avoid imposing upon him his own values and predilections. Undoubtedly, it was this objective, scientific approach, deeply rooted in Freud's personality and in his regard for the dignity of man, which enabled him to devise a method capable of overcoming the universal resistance to unburdening one's hidden secrets. Freud was a humanist in the noblest sense of the term.

At first glance it may seem paradoxical for a man who had dedicated himself to research to be the founder of a system of psychotherapy, but this contradiction is spurious and superficial. For Freud therapy and investigation were part of the same process. In fact, it is almost impossible to separate the history of the development of psychoanalytic technique from the history of the development of psychoanalytic theory. The evolution and refinement of Freud's psychoanalytic technique is a striking chapter in the history of scientific methodology. For the first time, a rational and consistent method of observing the manifestations of the human mind in a circumscribed, controlled fashion had been devised. The years which Freud spent in meticulous biological dissection and in carefully detailed microscopic observation had not been spent in vain.

In this section an attempt will be made to follow the evolution of Freud's ideas on psychotherapy by centering attention on what he felt to be the fundamental technical task at different phases of his psychoanalytic theories.

The prehistory of psychoanalysis goes back to hypnotism. Joseph Breuer had observed that when he placed a hysterical woman patient into a hypnotic trance and made her relate what was oppressing her mind at the moment, she would frequently tell of some highly affective fantasy or event in her life. When this experience was repeated with a discharge of emotion appropriate to the nature of the event the patient would be relieved of her symptoms. While awake the patient was completely unaware of the "traumatic" event or of its connection with her disability. For many years Freud carried with him the impression which this report of Breuer had made upon him. It was partially in pursuit of the therapeutic potential of hypnosis that he undertook studies first with Charcot at Paris and later with Bernheim and Liébault at Nancy. The former used hypnosis to reproduce in their minutest detail the symptoms of hysteria. The school at Nancy went even further; they used hypnosis for the purpose of curing the symptoms of hysteria. The essential feature of the cure, they felt, was the element of suggestion. When he returned to Vienna, Freud repeated Breuer's investigations and was satisfied that his results established their competence and validity.

In their joint publications concerning the origin of hysterical symptoms Breuer and Freud reasoned as follows: the symptoms of hysteria are the effects of an undischarged quantity of emotion, affect or excitation connected with a painful memory. Normally such memories are not pathogenic because the quantity of emotion connected with them is either discharged in conscious psychological reactions (abreacted) or is gradually integrated by assimilation or associative mental operations. In hysteria these reactions do not take place because the painful memories have been split off from their connection with the rest of the psyche. They are in a state of repression; they may be said to be unconscious. Recalling the traumatic events alone during hypnotic treatment was not sufficient to effect a cure. Discharge of an appropriate amount of excitation or emotion was necessary. The task of therapy, they concluded, was clearly to achieve the *catharsis* of the undischarged affect. It was his awareness of this formulation of the therapeutic task which led Freud to say that hysterics suffered mainly from reminiscences.

The differences between Breuer and Freud as to how the painful memories in hysteria had been rendered unconscious foreshadowed in part the next development in Freud's therapeutic technique. As already indicated, Breuer's explanation was a "physiological" one, in keeping with theories of hysteria current at the time. The memory of the traumatic event, he suggested, was split off from the rest of the mind because the event had taken place while the patient was in a hypnoid state. Freud favored a psychological theory. Traumatic events are forgotten or excluded from consciousness precisely because the individual seeks to defend himself from the pain attendant upon their recollection. It was this defensive resistance of the mind to such recollections that eventuated in repression. Apparently an important motive serving the interests of the conscious ego was involved, yet it was exactly this agency of the mind which was circumvented, which did not participate in the hypnotically induced recollection of the traumatic event. Working independently now, Freud conceived of the therapeutic task as the overcoming of resistances in order to undo the effect of repression. Hypnosis proved far from effective in this respect. Not all patients were amenable to hypnosis and many who were did not seem to go into a trance sufficiently deep for significant results. Such results as were obtained proved too ephemeral and the dependence upon the hypnotist too intense. At this point Freud's appreciation of the dynamic unconscious helped him to evolve a suitable technical substitute for hypnosis. He recalled an experiment which he had witnessed while with Bernheim. In his "Autobiographical Study" (1925) Freud described the incident in these words, "When the subject awoke from the state of somnambulism he seemed to have lost all memory of what had happened while he was in that state. But Bernheim maintained that the memory was present all the same; and if he insisted on the subject remembering, if he asseverated that the subject knew it all and had only to say it, and if at the same time he laid his hand on the subject's forehead, then the forgotten memories used in fact to return, hesitatingly at first but eventually in a flood and with complete clarity." In this manner Freud abandoned hypnosis in favor of a new technique, a technique of *forced associations,* of recollection carried out at the insistent demand of the therapist.

This technical innovation coincided with another interest which pervaded Freud's thoughts at the time. He had found that two elements were characteristic of the forgotten traumatic event to which he had been able to trace the hysterical symptoms. In the first place, these incidents invariably proved to be sexual in nature. Hysteria resulted from the conflict between the patient's sexual impulses and the resistances to sexuality. Second, in searching for the pathogenic situations in which the repression of sexuality had set in, he was carried further and further back into the patient's life, reaching ultimately into the earliest years of childhood, i.e., before the age of puberty when sexuality was supposed to begin. It is highly probable that in addition to the other factors already mentioned, the "error" of the seduction theory of the etiology of neurosis may in part be ascribed to the strong component of suggestion which Freud used in his technique of forced associations. In any event these early crucial sexual experiences of childhood were shrouded in what Freud called "infantile amnesia," and his emphasis in therapy now shifted from the cathartic effect of abreaction to the task of undoing this infantile amnesia.

From the methodological point of view the next development in psychoanalytic technique was by far the most momentous. Freud's personal analysis made it clear to him that in the seduction theory he had in fact stumbled upon the oedipus complex and infantile sexuality. Reports of his patients which he had taken at face value as historical truths were fantasies originating in these basic drives. To the operational concept of the dynamic unconscious he now added the principle of strict psychic determinism. He reduced the element of suggestion to a minimum in his new technical procedures and instead asked his patients to say freely and without criticism whatever came into their minds. The technique of *free association* had been evolved. Because the contents of the Unconscious had a dynamic propelling quality pressing for discharge, they inevitably manifested their effects by attaching themselves to derivatives or substitutive expressions which appear in consciousness as allusions, fragments, disguises and hints—as the elements of a dream become organized under the influence of the unconscious wish. It now became the task of the analyst to interpret this material, using principles very similar to dream interpretation. The scientific advantages of this new method were enormous. All aspects of the structure of the neurosis could be observed. The ego of the patient was in closer contact with the therapeutic process and with his actual current situation. Above all, the field of operations was kept relatively free of artifacts introduced by the analyst. Freud very correctly considered the introduction of free association as the beginning of psychoanalysis as a science.

After 1908 the period of Freud's "splendid isolation" was over. Physicians from various parts of Europe and America had become interested in his methods and were eager to put them into practice. Between 1912 and 1915 Freud wrote a series of papers on the subject of psychoanalytic technique, making clear the essentials of his method. In these publications he stressed the importance of one of the most striking features of psychotherapeutic experience: the very unique, highly emotional attitude which the patient develops toward the analyst —*transference*. Instead of recoiling in fear from the manifestations of transference Freud analyzed it. That he was able to avoid this pitfall to personal vanity and that he could understand transference phenomena as latter-day repetitions of the early history of his patients is perhaps the greatest index to Freud's scientific objectivity. Freud was very explicit in what he meant by the word "transference" as a repetition of the individual's early attitudes toward objects in the past. In spite of this the concept of transference has been widely misunderstood, vulgarized and misinterpreted. Because of the element of exquisite repetition the analysis of

transference became one of the most potent therapeutic tools for laying bare the conflicts of early
childhood and for helping the analyst undo the infantile amnesia. To this day transference analysis
has remained one of the cornerstones of psychoanalytic technique.

Before many years the young psychoanalytic
movement had matured sufficiently to suffer several
schisms. The most outstanding of the early deviants
were Jung and Adler, who differed with Freud on
fundamental questions of theory as well as technique. In order to keep the record clear for posterity Freud, in 1914, wrote "The History of the
Psychoanalytic Movement." In it he gave an account of the development of psychoanalysis, tracing
with utmost care how his method of treatment
evolved and how it differed from the views promul-
gated by Jung and Adler. The essentials of psychoanalysis, he maintained, were the theories of resistance and repression, the dynamic unconscious, the
etiological significance of the sexual factor, and the
importance of infantile experiences. The practices
of the deviants which he felt constituted contam-
inations of the scientific methods of psychoanalysis
placed them out of the bounds of the school of
thought which he had founded.

The theoretical implications of the technical
procedures he employed were never far from
Freud's mind. One of the considerations which led
him to revise his earlier concepts of mental func-

tioning and to introduce the structural hypothesis of the psychic apparatus was the phenomenon of *resistance,* which he encountered in therapeutic work. Resistance was unconscious and at the same time not directly a derivative of the instincts. Freud recognized resistance as an unconscious portion of the ego operating primarily to fend off the emergence of the unpleasant affect of anxiety. In *Inhibition, Symptom and Anxiety* (1926—the American translation is entitled *The Problem of Anxiety*) Freud brought his therapeutic techniques into consonance with his newly formulated structural conceptualization of the psyche. He introduced another nodal point of technical interest—the analysis of the operations of the ego. One may cite this change to illustrate the mutual influence of advances in theory and technique in Freud's psychoanalytic thinking. In demonstrating the defensive operations of the ego in warding off anxiety, he came to the conclusion that the affect of anxiety constituted a warning signal alerting the ego to the danger of emerging instinctual impulses. Anxiety was not a transmuted form of the libido, as he had thought previously, but an affect utilized by the ego as a warning signal against derivatives of either libidinal or aggressive drives. The analysis of resistances and defenses together with that of the transference occupy the foreground in modern psychoanalytic technique.

[ 57 ]

Despite the fact that it was a form of therapy forever linked to his name, Freud's evaluation of psychoanalysis was realistic and most conservative. The goal of analysis, he said, was to transform neurotic suffering into everyday misery. He warned against unrealistic magical anticipations from psychoanalytic treatment, and in the closing years of his life he was still evaluating in a critical way the therapeutic and methodological limitations of psychoanalysis. In "Analysis Terminable and Interminable" (1937) he reviewed the therapeutic process in psychoanalysis with a view to examining how it might be shortened, and in an effort to establish what criteria might be used for a satisfactory termination point of treatment. His conclusions reflected the vigorous objectivity so characteristic of Freud. The influence of reality, the structure of the patient's ego, and the personality of the analyst—all had to be taken into account in judging what one may anticipate from psychoanalysis. Freud did not minimize the importance of the personality of the analyst in evaluating the outcome of therapy. He recognized that the struggle against the unconscious forces of the mind is a never-ending one, and for that reason he urged analysts who have to cope with this problem as part of their everyday work to undergo periodic reanalysis. As a method of therapy he remarked analysis "ought not be despised."

To demonstrate Freud's constant awareness of

the problems of scientific methodology in psychoanalysis one may cite another publication of this period, "Constructions in Psychoanalysis" (1938). During treatment a considerable portion of the undoing of the childhood amnesia is not accomplished by direct recollection on the part of the patient. A certain degree of "reconstruction" of childhood experiences by the analyst is necessary. What were the methodological limitations of such constructions in psychoanalysis, and by what criteria could they be validated? These were some of the questions which Freud attempted to solve in this publication. He collected a set of typical responses to constructions in the analytic situation and examined their value for validating interpretations. For Freud the analytic situation constituted a laboratory for observing data and checking hypotheses.

# 8.

# *Contributions to Aesthetics*

W‍HILE it is hard to speculate which attributes of a genius determine the specific form which his creativity will take, it is difficult to conceive of the discoverer of psychoanalysis without thinking of a person of the richest possible background in literature, art, and the humanities. Freud held the creative artist in highest esteem. Psychoanalysis, he felt, could not elucidate the nature of the artistic gift nor explain the secret of artistic technique, but through a study of the unconscious it could establish the connections between the artist's life, his works and the vicissitudes of those impulses in him which he shared with all men. The transmutations, disguises and sublimations of the unconscious infantile wishes, especially those stemming from the oedipus complex, Freud had examined with utmost precision in his *Interpretation of Dreams*. Allusions to literature and representations of works of art were constant elements in the manifest dream or in the work of association during dream analysis. It is not surprising, therefore, that in the decades immediately following the publication of *The Inter-pretation of Dreams* Freud wrote many studies in which he applied psychoanalysis to the study of aesthetics. This section contains representative samplings of Freud's writings on wit, literature, art, and pathography.

In 1905 Freud published *Jokes and Their Rela-tion to the Unconscious.* This book is considered by many as his major contribution to the field of aesthetics. It grew out of a comment by Fliess that many of Freud's interpretations of dreams sounded like jokes, bad ones at that. Freud took this remark seriously and proceeded to collect and study jokes. In them he discovered the operation of mechanisms and disguises identical with those employed in dreams. Jokes are compromise formations discharg-ing either erotic or aggressive drives before an audience in a distorted fashion which temporarily overcomes the "censorship." The function of jokes is to achieve pleasure, and they take us back to the earlier periods of our life when, as children, we could enjoy pleasurable play untroubled by the demands of logic or reality. The book on jokes and their relation to the unconscious was the starting point for many psychoanalytic studies of wit and the comic.

Freud used the daydream as his point of depar-ture for the study of literature. Throughout the productions of neurotic patients, in their dreams, symptoms, and even in their life history, a leitmotiv frequently could be discerned, an organizing, integrating principle that seemed to give a pattern to the totality of the personality. This, Freud came to see, was the expression of a fantasy, the vehicle of some unconscious infantile wish. The fantasy could either be the creation of the patient's own imagination or borrowed from the creative artistry of some writer, in which case the patient was identifying himself with some character in a literary romance. Clearly, fantasy was the point of affinity between the processes of dream and symptom formation and the creative activity of the artist.

An admirable opportunity to explore and illustrate his theses came when he read the novel *Gradiva* by the Scandinavian writer, W. Jensen. In a psychological analysis of this novel which appeared in 1907 under the title "Delusions and Dreams in Jensen's *Gradiva*" Freud showed how the structure of the dreams, of the plot and of the delusions from which the central figure of the story suffered corresponded in every respect to the structure of fantasies, dreams and symptoms as encountered in psychoanalytic practice. The mechanisms of displacement, condensation, symbolization, representation by the opposite, etc., so familiar in spontaneous psychopathological formations, could all be detected in the "artificial" illness and dreams which Jensen had composed. In correspondence with the author Freud was able to ascertain that his interpretation of the novel was congruent with the intention of the author. Another field of human culture was now open to the probings of Freud's psychoanalytic method.

But what is the significance of the poet's intuitive grasp of the common conflicts of mankind? What are the dynamics of his creativity and how does he differ from the neurotic? These questions Freud undertook to answer the following year in his essay "The Relation of the Poet to Daydreaming." At the core of the poet's creativity is his private fantasy, his propensity to daydream which he shares with all men. The realm of imagination, Freud wrote, was a sanctuary established during the process of growing up in order to provide a substitute gratification for the narcissistic and instinctual wishes which have to be given up in real life. The artist, like the neurotic, withdraws from an unsatisfying reality into the world of imagination. Unlike the neurotic, however, the artist, through the exercise of his talents, finds his way back to the world of objects and to the gratifications afforded by reality. His private fantasy, embellished and modified by his artistic gift, disguised and distorted in order to avoid conflict with the forces of repression, he now shares with his audience. In addition to the technical qualities of formal beauty, the secret of the appeal of the poet's work resides in the fact that he has given formal yet acceptable expression to suppressed wishes of the members of his audience. They intuitively grasp the unconscious wish behind the elaborated fantasy and, through a process of identification with the poet or his representative in the fantasy, they achieve the pleasure which accrues from discharge of their pent-up instinctual wishes. The poet is the daydreamer for the community. The wishes and fantasies of the neurotic, on the other hand, remain his private problem and the conflicts over them he resolves privately through the process of symptom formation.

If the creations of artists were indeed analogous to the symptoms and fantasies of neurotics, it would seem correct to suppose that the psychoanalytic study of their works correlated with the material available concerning the artists could throw light on the psychology and the characteristic manner in which artists resolve their instinctual conflicts. A hint gleaned from the analysis of a patient gave Freud insight into the personality and works of Leonardo da Vinci. With characteristic concentration, Freud threw himself into the effort which resulted in one of his most highly polished, charming and erudite works. It was Freud's first attempt at pathography, the study of the unconscious motivations and development of an artist through an analysis of his life and works. Pathography constitutes a psychoanalytic form of aesthetic criticism. Its specific contribution is the addition of the dimension of depth, the psychology of the unconscious.

Freud's psychoanalytic biography of Leonardo da Vinci began with the analysis of a striking memory, the only childhood recollection which Leonardo ever recorded. The memory is so unusual that it arouses the suspicion that it was in fact a fantasy or a screen memory. Leonardo tells of a bird flying into his cradle and working its tail to and fro in his mouth. From the patent connection between this memory, the nursing situation and the symbolic significance of the bird, Freud pursued the analysis of Leonardo step by step until he shed a penetrating light upon the nature of the artist's sexuality, his creative and scientific life, and the specific features of some of his artistic works. Freud felt that the enjoyment of a work of art was not spoiled by the knowledge gained from such analysis. In subsequent years this form of psychoanalytic biography has been applied by many analysts and critics to significant personalities in literature and history.

The personality and historic image of the great Jewish leader, Moses, intrigued Freud throughout his life. No piece of statuary ever made a greater impression upon him than Michelangelo's heroic representation of Moses with the tablets of the law. The awesome admiration which this great work inspired in Freud puzzled him and aroused his curiosity, ". . . I am no connoisseur in art but simply a layman. Nevertheless, works of art exercise a powerful effect upon me, especially those of literature and sculpture, less often of painting. This has occasioned me, when I have been contemplating such things, to spend a long time before them trying to apprehend them in my own way, that is, to explain to myself what their effect is due to. Wherever I cannot do this, as for instance with music, I am incapable of obtaining any pleasure. Some rationalistic or perhaps analytic turn of mind in me rebels against being moved by a thing without knowing why I am thus affected and what it is that affects me."

With these words Freud set out to unravel the secret of the grandeur of the "Moses of Michelangelo" (1914). No detail of the statue escaped his meticulous scrutiny—the position of the fingers, the folds of the beard, and the upturned tablets of the law. Every facet of the composition was the starting point for a train of thought leading to an awareness of the deeper feelings which the statue aroused in the beholder. In the end Freud felt he understood what it was in the statue that had moved him so much. It was indeed a concrete expression of a moment of immense grandeur—a representation of the fulfillment "of the highest mental achievement that is possible in a man—that of struggling successfully against an inward passion for the sake of a cause to which he has devoted himself." For to Freud the details of the statue portrayed an attitude which is not recorded in the Bible. This was not a wrathful leader, smashing the tablets in a fit of rage, but the hero of self-mastery who curbs his immediate passions to preserve for his people the laws of morality, unworthy though his people may be to receive them. It can hardly be doubted that in many respects Freud felt a strong sense of identification with Moses.

None of Freud's forays into the realm of applied psychoanalysis was devoid of its clinical significance. In the pathography of Leonardo da Vinci, for example, he described the genetics of a specific form of homosexuality. In a similar study of Dosstoevsky ("Dostoevsky and Parricide"—1928) he showed how criminality, gambling and certain forms of convulsive seizures develop out of the conflicts of the oedipal period.

It was the weakness of Dostoevsky's moral position which impressed itself upon Freud. "After the most violent struggles to reconcile the instinctual demands of the individual with the claims of the community, he [Dostoevsky] landed in the retrograde position of submission both to temporal and spiritual authority, of veneration both for the Tsar and for the God of the Christians, and of a narrow Russian nationalism—a position which lesser minds have reached with smaller effort. This is the weak point in that great personality. Dostoevsky threw away the chance of becoming a teacher and liberator of humanity and made himself one with their gaolers. The future of human civilization will have little to thank him for. It seems probable that he was condemned to this failure by his neurosis. The greatness of his intelligence and the strength of his love for humanity might have opened to him another, an apostolic, way of life."

Dostoevsky's neurosis, Freud suggested, arose out of an inability to master feelings of guilt over unresolved infantile parricidal wishes. The stories he wrote about his characters and the tragedies he arranged in his own life reflected a need for punishment, a compulsion to suffer in order to expiate the unconscious primal crime of mankind, parricide. In the account of how Dostoevsky kept gambling and losing, Freud saw a pattern of alternating sin and penance. Immense literary talent and boundless love for humanity did not achieve for Dostoevsky the essence of morality, which is renunciation. The great leader, such as Moses was, must be master of his impulses.

# 9.

## *The Study of Religion*

THE stories of the Bible, Freud wrote, moved him deeply when a child. The atmosphere of his home was liberal regarding religious doctrine and in no sense stringent concerning ritual. Freud, it seems, was at one with those late nineteenth-century intellectuals, international in outlook, above superstition and prejudice, who posited their faith in rationalism, in the progress of civilization through the advance of science. Science was the only firm basis for his *Weltanschauung*, Freud said in the last of his *New Introductory Lectures*.

The universality of the oedipus complex and the ubiquity of its manifold derivatives—these were at the roots of Freud's contribution to the study of religion. His approach was at the opposite pole from Jung's. The latter used his vast knowledge of mythology and comparative religion in an effort to elucidate the problem of neurosis. So uncertain a basis could hardly appeal to Freud. More mindful than Jung of scientific methodology, Freud drew his conclusions from his clinical work, from his observations on patients, applying what he

[ 69 ]

learned to the broader problems of religion and mythology.

The classic case histories of "Little Hans" ("Analysis of a Phobia in a Five-Year-Old Boy"—1909) and the "Rat Man" ("Notes upon a Case of Obsessional Neurosis"—1909) demonstrate the kind of clinical material and the nature of the data upon which Freud based his truly revolutionary analysis of the origin of religion. Hans was a little boy who would not go into the street for fear that a horse would bite him. The analysis revealed that the horse represented a substitute for the father whose bite the young patient feared in retaliation for incestuous and parricidal wishes. The fear and awe of children suffering from zoophobia resemble the attitude of certain primitive peoples toward their totem animals. If the feared object of the animal phobia stood for the father, could not the same be true in the case of the totem animal?

In an earlier paper, "Obsessional Acts and Religious Practices" (1907), Freud made what seemed passing reference to the similarity between the neurotic structures created to fend off the return of wishes unsuccessfully renounced and the ritualistic practices characteristic of many religions. Religion as a social institution is also founded on the need to effect the renunciation of asocial impulses. He concluded that the obsessional patient creates what is in effect a private religion, a kind of caricature of established religions. Religion, on the other hand, he said, was the universal obsessional neurosis of mankind. ✗

In the study of the "Rat Man" Freud discerned mental processes and symptoms which clearly had their counterpart in the practices of primitive peoples. Foremost among these were the use of magical thinking, the respect for certain taboos, and the compulsion to perform certain rituals. Primitive beliefs and the unconscious fantasies of neurotics often bear a striking similarity. The persistence of a taboo indicated the operation of a strong wish, a temptation which could not be overcome except by avoidance or by the invocation of superstitious dread. This attitude could be accounted for, as in the case of the obsessional neurotic, by the coexistence of opposing feelings, i.e., ambivalence. The compulsive act or ritual is a magical method for resolving the delicate balance between the unconscious wish and the forces of repression. The unconscious wish involved in the obsessional neurosis consists of the incestuous and parricidal impulses of the oedipus complex. The next step obviously was to determine whether the same was true for the taboos and rituals of totemistic religions. Freud was impressed by the striking correspondence between the two major taboo injunctions of totemism (not to kill the totem, not to have sexual relations with any woman of the same totem clan) and the two elements of the oedipus complex (killing the father and taking the mother to wife). By identify-

[ 71 ]

✗ In later yrs Freud felt religion contained a truth concerning prehistory of human race. Religion symbolically recapitulated the outcome of a primordial struggle between authority of the father & the mother clan.

ing the totem animal as the symbol for the father of
the clan, Freud could explain totemism and exog-
amy as socially institutionalized structures for overcoming the two basic wishes of the oedipus
complex, parricide and incest.

Having progressed to this point, an even more
dramatic component of totemistic religion, the
totem feast, could be brought into relation with the
vicissitudes of the oedipus complex. Once a year,
the totem animal, which at other times is regarded
as sacred, is solemnly killed, communally devoured
and mourned over. Immediately afterwards a period of triumphant rejoicing supervenes during
which the taboos, honored throughout the year, are
communally abrogated. At the end of this period
the taboos are re-established, the totem is venerated
once again and the cycle of community life begins
anew. By substituting the image of the father for
the totem animal Freud could point out a striking
parallel to the development of the young child in
more highly civilized societies. During the oedipal
phase the little boy wants to supplant his father
and have his mother. He wishfully fantasies killing
the father, devouring him and thereby becoming
privy to his prowess and sexual prerogative. Overcome by guilt, fear and remorse for the father
whom he also loves, the little boy ultimately puts
aside his parricidal impulses, renounces his desire
for the mother and begins to model himself after
the father. The father's prohibitions he now makes

his own, and the father's aggrandized image becomes the ideal toward which the boy aspires. The boy thus reaches the threshold of morality. The totem feast is a primeval re-enactment of the same fantasies of the oedipal phase or, as Freud said, a ritualistic recapitulation of an event from man's prehistoric past. This past Freud reconstructed as follows: originally, men lived in small hordes dominated by a single powerful father image who had access to all the women and power over all the younger and weaker rival males. One day the jealous sons united, killed and devoured their father, their enemy and also their ideal. "After the deed they were unable to take over the heritage since they stood in one another's way. Under the influence of failure and regret they learned to come to an agreement among themselves. They banded themselves into a clan of brothers by the help of the ordinances of totemism which aimed at the prevention of repetition of such a deed, and they jointly undertook to forego the possession of the women on whose account they had killed their father. . . . The totem feast was the commemoration of the fearful deed from which sprang man's sense of guilt (or original sin)." The image of the murdered primal father ultimately was elevated beyond the totem animal into the role of a distant deity endowed with ideal qualities and accorded infinite awe and reverence.

In this fashion Freud advanced a set of hypotheses which, for the first time, encompassed in a rational way the taboos of primitive man with the rituals of modern religion; the Eleusinian mysteries, the Dionysian rites and the Christian sacrament of communion; the organization of society with the myths and fears of childhood. The beginnings of religion, morality, social life and art, Freud wrote, all meet in the oedipus complex. The concepts elaborated in *Totem and Taboo* opened a new era in the study of comparative religion. Freud's brilliant psychoanalytic investigation of the origin of religion exposed the limitations of any attempt to account for the phenomenology of comparative religion which fails to take into account the unconscious mind.

The *Standard Edition* of Freud's Works lists twenty-six articles which he wrote on the subject of religion and related topics. The persistent recurrence of this subject in his writings is not surprising in the light of the tremendous role which religion plays in the life of civilized man and the variety of forms of religious experience.

The analysis of "A Neurosis of Demoniacal Possession in the Seventeenth Century" (1923) deserves mention at this point for several reasons. To begin with, this type of disturbance was not uncommon during the Middle Ages. A pact with the devil was considered a problem for the church or for the state; rarely was it regarded as a form of mental illness. In the second place, this "religious neurosis" differed from previous analyses of religious experiences. The neurosis of demoniacal possession was based on a negative, not a positive oedipal situation. The subject of the study, a man, was in conflict over a feminine, passive sexual wish for his father's love. In *Totem and Taboo* Freud had referred to the essentially submissive feminine attitude toward the God-father image implied in religion. In this case the sublimation of religion failed, and the passive feminine wishes became the basis for a neurosis. In later studies of group formation and hypnosis Freud returned to the influence of the role of sublimated homosexuality in the organization of society.

In *The Future of an Illusion* which Freud wrote in 1928 he was less concerned with the origin of religion than with the function of religion in the actual context of man's social existence. The influence of the concepts of narcissism and aggression, which he had developed in the meantime, is prominent in this work. Faced by the inevitability of personal extinction and sensing his powerlessness over the forces of nature, man seeks refuge regressively by reviving the image of the omnipotent and omniscient father of his childhood. The reward for submission and renunciation is participation in God's protecting might and the promise of eventual triumph over all narcissistic insults, especially death. Religious adherence also acts to strengthen the forces of repression in the individual and tends

[ 75 ]

to make bearable those necessary instinctual renunciations which make civilized life feasible. By accepting the universal obsessional neurosis of mankind, the individual is spared the task of forming a personal neurosis. Religious belief serves the function of a wish-fulfilling illusion, comforting but impractical in man's struggle against the powerful forces threatening him from within and from the external world without. For in the end all illusions must give way to knowledge and such is the fate in store for the communal, universal illusion of religion. It is possible, Freud said, for scientific work to discover something about the reality of the world through which we can increase our power and according to which we can regulate our lives.

These nonreligious sentiments of Freud did not distract him from his never-ending attempt to penetrate more deeply into the significance of religion in the life of man. Although his personal views were neither nationalistic nor religious, he felt a strong bond to his own people, the Jews, whose special position in the history of Western morality and whose unhappy fate at the hands of Hitler dramatized the challenging questions his searching intellect had posed. In *Moses and Monotheism* (1937), a highly daring and speculative work, Freud returned to the theme of one of his great heroes, Moses, and to the religion which he founded—monotheistic Judaism. Recognizing the limitations of his methodology, Freud nevertheless pursued relentlessly the analysis of the material available concerning the life of Moses, from his remarkable rescue by the daughter of Pharaoh shortly after birth to his mysterious death in the desert wastes beyond the Promised Land.

The scope of this book is most ambitious. In it Freud tried to effect a synthesis of the results of the widely ranging investigations he had conducted throughout his life. His goal was to explain the origin of monotheism, the character of the Jewish people, and their relation to the Christian world which has persecuted them so persistently. He returned to many of the themes advanced in *Totem and Taboo* but went far beyond them. There was a truth in religion, he concluded, not a material truth but a historical truth—a historical truth whose reverberations from the forgotten past are felt until the present day. Not one but two heroes named Moses existed in the history of the Jewish people. The first, a follower of the defeated monotheistic Pharaoh, Ikhnaton, was an Egyptian noble, just as the Bible story reads. It was he who "chose" and created the Jewish people, gave them their monotheistic ideal and the laws of morality and imposed upon them the grandeur of his character and his ideals of renunciation, spirituality and tenacity. It was also he who met the fate of the primal horde father, namely, to be murdered by his followers and later exalted as the God figure. The second Moses was a Midianite, in keeping with the many dualities and inconsistencies of the legends of the Bible concerning Moses. Applying the techniques of psychological analysis to historical movements, Freud traced the return of the primal crime of parricide from its historical repression and related it to the rise of the Messianic concept which ultimately eventuated in the Christian faith. Anti-Semitism is based on an *unconscious* reproach against the Jews, viz., "We admit we killed God; why don't you?"

The power of this religious memory to stretch across the centuries and to force the masses under its spell Freud considered truly astonishing. It could only be accounted for through, and in fact it demonstrates, the forcefulness of the repressed, dynamic potential in the unconscious mind of man. But even this psychological account of the origin of religion did not quite grasp its unique profundity. Freud wrote, "To all matters concerning the creation of a religion—and certainly to that of the Jewish one—pertains something which is majestic which has not so far been covered by our explanations. Some other element should have part in it; one that has few analogies and nothing quite like it; something unique and commensurate with that which has grown out of it; something like religion itself."

# 10.

## *Contributions to Mythology, Anthropology and Sociology*

To the serious reader of Freud no charge seems more incongruous than the assertion that he neglected the influence of society on human psychology. From the beginning of his career as a psychologist until the end Freud emphasized the interaction between man's biological endowment and the social setting which modifies, elaborates and gratifies his drives. Naturally at different phases of the development of his understanding Freud paid greater attention to one or another specific factor, in accord with the interest which was paramount at the time in his investigations. In fact, in his methodology, Freud did not separate man from his organic environment. He applied the same working concepts of genetic development, internal conflict and the dynamic effect of the (irrational) unconscious mind to individuals, to social institutions and to the development of society itself. While it is still too early to assess accurately the import of Freud's contributions to the social sciences, it is nevertheless obvious ever that the concepts just mentioned have been playing an increasingly greater role in sociological and anthropological literature. His description of the conflicts within the basic social unit— the family—and the effects of environmental pressures on the instinctual drives of the child opened a new era in the study of human interrelationships.

In this section on the study of man, perhaps more than in any other portion of this essay, it is difficult to assign the writings of Freud to definite compartments. In one way or another every one of his contributions advanced the knowledge of anthropology if we understand the term in its most comprehensive sense. For a generation raised in an era in which the ideas of Freud have wide currency it is hard to envisage how educators and sociologists could have formulated their tasks without an awareness of those forces in childhood which are most potent in the shaping of human personality, namely, the instincts and the impressions of the earliest years of life.

For social scientists and pedagogues whose work touches on the question of child rearing, character formation, education and national character, the novel discoveries which Freud described in the *Three Contributions to the Theory of Sex* (1905) and in the early papers on the formation of character are of the utmost importance. During the earlier period of his researches Freud was concerned, above all, with tracing various psychological manifestations to the effects of repressed libidinal impulses. Although the sexual development of the human infant tends to unfold in a pattern predetermined by his biological inheritance, the types of behavior which may develop in response to the stimulations or inhibitions of child-rearing practices are infinitely variable. Character traits develop out of permanent ego defenses set up against the derivatives of infantile sexuality. The types of pressures (punishment or reward) which the child-rearing practices of a specific culture bring to bear on the developing instincts of the child will in the long run influence the nature of the character structure of members of that society. The conflicts over infantile sexuality, especially the oedipal wishes, must be resolved in a fashion consistent with the ideals and standards of the particular community. The crucial years of personality formation are the first five to six years of life. It is only thereafter that the individual can turn from the domination by his instincts to the task of learning to master the external world. These early hypotheses of Freud have been substantiated by direct observation of children and have formed a valuable frame of reference for an ever-growing number of anthropological and cultural studies.

Comparative mythology is perhaps one of the most interesting and intriguing chapters in anthropology, and here too Freud utilized what he had learned about the structure and function of fantasy in mental life. The first myths that an individual invents he invents about himself. Often they constitute a wish-fulfilling re-edition of the events of the individual's childhood. Projected onto the heroes of the past, these fantasies become the basis of the universal myths of mankind—universal, because they are based on the childhood experiences common to all men. The poets of primeval times were the original mythmakers. Perhaps the most popular fantasy remembered from childhood is the one which holds that one is not truly the child of one's own parents,× but that, having been abandoned by parents of nobler lineage, one was raised by an inferior set of false parents. These fantasies, the precursor in the individual of the widely celebrated *Myth of the Birth of the Hero* (Otto Rank) Freud called "family romances" (1909). The family romance begins with the child's estrangement from his parents, usually as a result of disappointment over their failure to conform with his oedipal wishes. In the family romance the true parents are punitively denigrated and, by disavowing the blood relationship, the child is enabled to circumvent guilt feelings over incestuous wishes. Incorporated into the fabric of regional myths and associated with glorious figures of the nation's past, the repressed wishes of childhood may be indulged in communally and vicariously through an identification with the central figures of the myth. The psychology of the dream process made possible the

× Family Romances (1909) C.P. V

interpretation of the hidden meaning of myths, legends and fairy tales and the understanding of the secret of their immortal charm. Family romances are noteworthy in another, perhaps a minor, way. A statistical study undertaken to evaluate the correctness of psychoanalytic propositions demonstrated that eighty percent of the subjects could recall entertaining during childhood a fantasy of precisely this nature.

There is hardly a major clinical study by Freud in which some myth is not explained. Examples of such myths are stories of Prometheus, Medusa and, of course, Moses. ˣIn anthropological research psychoanalytic interpretations of myths have been used in many ways, especially as a method of elucidating the repressed infantile wishes of the members of primitive societies who cannot be investigated with psychoanalytic technique.

The quintessence of his early views on the psychological analysis of anthropological data Freud spelled out in *Totem and Taboo*. Besides explaining the origin of totemistic religion, which was his main purpose, Freud brought into meaningful relationship a host of primitive customs and beliefs. He accomplished this by pursuing unremittingly the analogy between the obsessional neurosis and the mind and manners of savages. The mental traits which place the pathognomonic stamp upon the psychology of obsessional neurosis—isolation, reaction formation, undoing, magical thinking, and

*1913*

ˣ In "Little Hans", the meaning of totem animal
In "Rat Man", interrelation between magic, ambivalence & taboo
in obsessional neurosis

intense ambivalence—all of these Freud pointed out in the customs of primitive peoples. An awareness of the existence of unconscious incestuous wishes was sufficient by itself to illuminate a whole set of taboos whose purpose was to shield primitive man from his awful dread of incest. The idea that social customs may have a purpose which may remain incomprehensible to the objective observer as well as to the subjective participant was a fresh and novel concept for anthropologists. The only kind of purpose which they had been accustomed to ascribe to the practices of primitive peoples was of the order of the so-called normal or rational motivations, e.g., prestige, economic and geographic considerations. It is impossible to exaggerate the magnitude of this contribution of Freud to the study of anthropology.

The large component of primary-process and magical thinking which is evident in the lives of primitives made it possible for Freud to draw many conclusions from their "manifest" behavior. In the treatment which such peoples accord their rulers, their enemies and the dead, Freud could point out undeniable proof of extreme ambivalence, a quality particularly characteristic of the aboriginal mind. The belief in the omnipotence of one's wishes, a discovery brought to light in the analysis of neurotics, clarified the power exerted over the savage by his dreams and devils, his spells and amulets, his magic and his mana. Thus it became pos-

sible to render intelligible the behavior of primitive people by placing it in the context of their
magical mode of thinking. Freud turned the same
unprejudiced objective eye on the behavior and
beliefs of primitive men as he had on the dreams
and neuroses of their more civilized cousins.

The earlier models for Freud's theoretical formulations were erected largely on the experience
derived from the psychoanalysis of men. Only later
did he come to appreciate what he called the psychological consequences of the anatomical distinc-
tion between the sexes. As he added to his knowledge of feminine psychology, he was impressed by
the unconscious hostility which pervaded the love
life of certain women. For them menarche, defloration and childbirth, the nodal points of female
biological development, symbolized being turned
into a woman, in a word—castration. The act of
defloration liberated in such women an archaic
enmity toward the man which may take the form
of the woman remaining bound to the man in a
perpetual thralldom of hate. She cannot free herself
from him because her revenge upon him is not yet
complete. Naturally, such marriages are hardly ever
happy ones; yet a surprisingly large number of
women who remain sexually anesthetic and unhappy throughout their first marriage often can
effect a happy second marriage during which they
manage to make another man happy. The second
husband who played no part whatsoever in the

defloration fares much better than the man who did. From these observations Freud could understand the function of the ritual of ceremonial defloration which is found among primitive peoples in many parts of the world. By having the priest or the elder of the tribe take upon himself in the name of the community the onus for deflowering the virgin before marriage, the future husband who presumably must live with the woman for the rest of his life is spared one of the important unconscious sources of unhappiness in marriage. In this short study, "The Taboo of Virginity" (1918), one may observe in cameo how Freud extrapolated from the data of clinical experience insights into problems of the broadest social application.

One of the first clinical and sociological applications of Freud's evolving ego psychology was a small but compact book on *Group Psychology and the Analysis of the Ego* (1921). He applied his knowledge of two sets of phenomena familiar to him from his clinical researches, namely, identification and hypnosis. Both processes entail powerful emotional bonds which connect one individual to another. These are the mechanisms which also come into play in the formation of groups. There is a powerful erotic tie which binds each individual member of the group to the leader. This tie constitutes the common element which enables the members of the group to identify themselves with each other, while the leader of the group fills the role of the collective ego ideal. What had previously been an intrapsychic relationship (the relation of the ego to its ideal) has now become an interpersonal relationship (the relation of the individual to the leader). Thus the relationship to the leader has a narcissistic origin. Onto the leader are projected all the ideal qualities toward whose realization the individual aspires in vain. To be effective, therefore, the leader must respond to the unconscious expectations of the mob. He must be distant and aloof, self-centered and independent, free from doubts and uncertainty, the epitomization of the childhood concept of the omnipotent and omniscient father. Endowed by the "mob mind" with such qualities, he cast over them his magical hypnotic spell. He is the descendant of the primal father whom the horde follows in blind obedience, wanting only to submit. He is the group ideal governing the ego in place of the individual's own ego ideal. In 1921 when Freud wrote this essay one could hardly have suspected that within a decade Germany would be well on the way toward being engulfed by the frightful Nazi tyranny, a despotism which exemplified in the most extreme fashion the archaic and irrational ties to the primal horde leader. This analysis of group formation which at the time of its publication seemed so esoteric unfortunately received an all too convincing verification from the final arbiter in such matters, the course of history itself.

Freud, however, had neither prophecies nor panaceas to offer. In *Civilization and Its Discontents* (1930) he took cognizance of the inevitable conflict between man's biological impulses and the process of civilization. For culture to develop and advance, progressive renunciation of direct gratification of the instincts by members of the society is an unavoidable requirement. Not all members of society are equally capable of this, and unhappiness and discontent, manifest in many forms, are inevitable. The aggressive drives in particular present a hazard. Too great a degree of externalization or internalization of these drives spells out baleful dangers for the safety of the state or the health of the individual. Replying to a letter from Albert Einstein Freud returned to this question in *Why War?* (1933). In a period when men have perfected destructive techniques capable of putting an end to either or both sides in a war, such hope as there is for peace must be sought in the psychological qualities characteristic of cultural advance and attainment, viz., "a strengthening of the intellect, which is beginning to govern instinctual life and an internalization of the aggressive impulses with all its consequent advantages and perils." War is the crassest opposition to the psychical attitude imposed by the cultural process, yet only the élite in human society has achieved to any marked degree a psychical attitude in consonance with culture; and time, Freud felt, may be running out too fast for the mass of

[ 88 ]

x  7 felt abolition of war ~~ran into~~ as an instrument of national relations ran into firm obstacle of the aggression inherent in human nature. He hoped the ability of ego to master the primitive drives of id could serve as a hopeful model in international relations

o  This book has become standard text for advanced students in Sociology in many universities. In it 7 emphasizes how intersection society to reach the necessary level of cultural and psychological integration. In the meantime, only a modest goal could be placed before the true pacifist —whatever fosters the growth of culture works at the same time against war. What little optimism a man freed from illusions could cling to was based on the model of the psychic apparatus of the individual. After severe struggles the ego can attain mastery over the primitive drives of the id. Could some analogous rationality perhaps assume the ascendancy in international affairs?

between instinctual demands of individual & strictures of social order lead inevitably to progress & discontent.

# 11.

## Freud's Literary Style

Not the least of Freud's gifts was his great literary talent, an ability to convey his novel and often complicated concepts in clear and simple language. The style of his published scientific works was restrained and proper. Rarely did he deviate from his expository goal for the sake of stylistic effect. In *The Interpretation of Dreams* he presented a considerable body of very personal data, all subordinated to the scientific task that he had set for himself, namely, an explanation of dream analysis. In his letters to Fliess (*The Origins of Psychoanalysis*) which Marie Bonaparte saved and preserved for posterity and which were published posthumously, one can observe, however, quite a different aspect of his style—a light and witty trend, a restless rapid tempo with occasional bursts of despair and lyricism. In a letter dated March 11, 1902 Freud gave a humorous account of how he achieved one of his lifelong ambitions, to be appointed Professor at the University of Vienna. The rank was finally bestowed upon Freud through the intercession of influential friends. In the excerpt which follows Freud describes to Fliess how he and his household responded to the good news.

"The *Wiener Zeitung* has not yet published it, but the news spread quickly from the Ministry. The public enthusiasm is immense. Congratulations and bouquets keep pouring in, as if the role of sexuality had been suddenly recognized by His Majesty, the interpretation of dreams confirmed by the Council of Ministers, and the necessity of the psycho-analytic therapy of hysteria carried by a two-thirds majority in Parliament.

"I have obviously become reputable again and my shyest admirers now greet me from a distance in the street.

"I myself would still gladly exchange five congratulations for one good case coming for extensive treatment. . . .

"In the whole affair there is one person with very long ears, who was not sufficiently allowed for in your letter, and that is myself. If I had taken those few steps three years ago I should have been appointed three years earlier, and should have spared myself much. Others are just as clever, without having to go to Rome first."

The reference to Rome was probably an allusion to one of Freud's inhibitions which he had overcome in self-analysis. For years Freud had wanted to visit the Eternal City but always found some difficulty in carrying through his wish. In *The Interpretation of Dreams* he indicates that visiting Rome was the symbol of the achievement of an unconscious, guilt-laden childhood ambition, and he remarks in a footnote that wishes are not so difficult to realize if one has the courage to pursue his goal.

The fundamental rule of psychoanalytic technique brought under Freud's surveillance the most intimate details of the private lives of his patients, yet throughout his case histories and clinical studies there is no trace of suggestiveness or condescension nor the slightest breach of good taste. He imparted an air of dignity and elegance to whatever subject he described. Freud had the felicitous gift of finding or coining the precise word he required to express his thoughts. Even his most compact presentations he endowed with a sense of grace. Under the rather unexciting title "A Special Type of Object Choice Made by Men" (1910) in a few short pages Freud described one of the commonest fantasies in the love life of men—the rescue fantasy. The age-old motif of rescuing a woman from danger and thereby winning her love is the essence of innumerable myths, poems, stories and even religious traditions. A very special elaboration of this theme involves "the love of a man for a harlot," a factor which Freud observed as a special condition for love in several of his male patients. The feature of saving the fallen woman introduces an element of moral elevation which lends poignancy and tragedy to some of the greatest masterpieces of literature. The ramifications of this theme are endless. Thais, Sadie Thompson and Mary Magdalene are relatively undisguised examples of such heroines; and for the man, the element of playing the redeeming saviour may be expressed in almost any form of activity—adventure, the choice of profession, or vicariously, in a religious myth. In an astonishing feat of condensation Freud combined all the elements of the myths with the essential features in the psychology of his patients and showed the universal unconscious identity of rescuing and giving a child. In a few sentences he could summarize the harvest of what must have been months of analytic toil, and in the case of this contribution to the psychology of love he did so with a delicacy and charm appropriate to the nature of his subject.

This was part of Freud's genius, to be able to capture from his patients' conflicts a theme universal in the emotional experience of mankind and to find for it an apt and beautiful allusion from the rich storehouse of his reading. The significance of analogous representations in literature, on the other hand, intrigued him as well and stimulated him to search out their common unconscious meanings. "The Theme of the Three Caskets" (1913) portrays this aspect of Freud's gift at its very best. There are many stories in which the hero is called upon to make a choice between three women. Classically he selects the youngest who also remains silent. Why does the victory belong to the silent one, the youngest of the three? The solution of the problem came through the use of mechanisms so familiar in the interpretation of dreams. If silence is taken as the representation of death and the roles of the characters are reversed, one may say that what is symbolized is the three inevitable relations which man has with woman—"that with the mother who bears him, with the companion of his bed and board and with the destroyer. Or it is the three forms taken on by the figure of the mother as life proceeds: the mother herself, the beloved who is chosen after her pattern and finally the mother Earth who receives him again. But it is in vain that the old man yearns after the love of woman as once he had it from his mother; the third of the Fates alone, the silent goddess of death will take him into her arms. . . . Eternal wisdom in the garb of the primitive myth bids the old man renounce love, choose death and make friends with the necessity of dying."

Freud rarely addressed himself to the general public. On those occasions when he did he slackened neither his literary tastes nor his scientific standards for the purpose of popularity. For a number of years Freud gave a course of lectures at the University of Vienna. Originally the audience consisted of three people; ultimately it grew to more than one hundred. Freud spoke freely, intimately, and without notes. Out of this experience grew the book *Introductory Lectures on Psychoanalysis*

(1917). Freud transmitted to the printed page the informality and sense of intimacy of the lecture platform. The first two sections of the book, those on the psychopathology of everyday life and dreams, were delivered without being written in advance. They were set down in writing accurately afterwards thanks to what Freud called his gift of phonographic memory. These lectures are models of lucidity, clarity and organization. Taking a new and complicated field of knowledge, Freud developed his thesis step by step, beginning with simple, acceptable, common-sense concepts and advancing his argument consistently until the new and startling ideas which he had to place before his audience seemed like the inevitable, logical consequences of each individual's own cogitation. The *Introductory Lectures on Psychoanalysis* remains to this day, perhaps, the easiest and most direct approach to the understanding of psychoanalysis.

In 1930 the city of Frankfort bestowed on Freud the singular honor of awarding him the Goethe prize. In a letter informing Freud of this action the secretary of the Board of Judges stated, "According to the rules covering the bestowal of the Goethe prize it is to be given to the personality whose work has been generally recognized and whose creative efforts are worthy of being honored in memory of Goethe.

"By bestowing the prize on you the Board wishes to express the high value which it attributes to the revolutionary effects of the new forms of research created by you on the formative forces of our time. By strictly scientific methods and by simultaneously boldly interpreting the parables coined by poets your research built a new access to the driving forces of the soul and made it possible to understand the origin and structure of many forms of culture in their roots, and to heal illnesses for which the medical profession did not possess the keys until now. Your psychology, however, did not only revolutionize and enrich medical science but also the world of images, of artists, ministers, of historians and educators. . . ."

To Freud this was the climax of his life as a citizen. In the acceptance speech which was read for him by his daughter Anna, Freud indicated how much it meant for him to have his name linked with one of the truly great bearers of universal culture.

"Soon afterward," wrote Freud, "the boundaries of our country narrowed and the nation would know no more of us." But the writings of Freud which the Nazis saw fit to consign to the fires of their destruction have survived to become a legacy for all mankind.